"There was one of two things I had a right to, liberty, or death; if I could not have one, I would have the other; for no man should take me alive; I should fight for my liberty as long as my strength lasted, and when the time came for me to go, the Lord would let them take me."

– Harriet Tubman

HARRIET ROSS TUBMAN

BY DON TROY

The Child's World®

GRAPHIC DESIGN
Robert E. Bonaker / Graphic Design & Consulting Co.

PROJECT COORDINATOR
James R. Rothaus / James R. Rothaus & Associates

EDITORIAL DIRECTION
Elizabeth Sirimarco

PHOTO RESEARCH
Ann Schwab / The Child's World, Inc.

COVER PHOTO
Portrait of Harriet Ross Tubman / Corbis-Bettmann

CURRICULUM COORDINATOR
Cynthia Klingel / Curriculum Director, School District #77, Mankato, MN

Library of Congress Cataloging-in-Publication Data
Troy, Don
Harriet Ross Tubman / by Don Troy.
p. cm
Includes index.
Summary: A biography of the black woman whose cruel
experiences as a slave in the South led her to seek
freedom in the North for herself and for others
through the Underground railroad.
ISBN 1-56766-568-3 (library reinforced : alk. paper)

1. Tubman, Harriet, 1820?-1913 — Juvenile literature.
2. Slaves —United States — Biography— Juvenile literature.
3. Afro-Americans — Biography — Juvenile literature.
4. Underground railroad — Juvenile literature.
5. Antislavery movements —United States — Juvenile literature.
[1. Tubman, Harriet, 1820?-1913. 2. Slaves. 3. Afro-Americans —
Biography. 4. Women — Biography. 5. Underground railroad.]
I. Title. II. Series.

E444.T82T76 1999   98-26879
305.5'67'092 — dc21   CIP
[B]   AC

Contents

A Child Slave

When Harriet Tubman was born, her name was Araminta Ross. She was a *slave,* just as her parents were. No records were kept of slave births, so Araminta never knew how old she was. She was born in either 1820 or 1821 in Maryland, only 100 miles south of Pennsylvania — a state where it was illegal to own slaves.

A man named Edward Brodas owned Araminta and her 11 brothers and sisters. Their grandparents had been born free on the African continent, but then they were kidnapped. They were crowded onto a ship with hundreds of other Africans, brought to America, and sold as slaves. Once a person became a slave, their children and grandchildren were usually forced into slavery as well.

Like most *African American* slaves, Araminta's large family lived in the poorest of conditions. Their one-room cabin had no windows or furniture. There was an open cooking fire in the center of the room. The children slept on straw tossed on the dirt floor, huddled close to the fire to stay warm. Harriet had no shoes and few clothes. Food was cornmeal mush, or sometimes sweet potatoes from her mother's garden. Her family was allowed the privilege of hunting and fishing, so occasionally they had meat as well.

Negroes for Sale.

A Cargo of very fine stout Men and Women, in good order and fit for immediate service, just imported from the Windward Coast of Africa, in the Ship Two Brothers.— Conditions are one half Cash or Produce, the other half payable the first of January next, giving Bond and Security if required.

The Sale to be opened at 10 o'Clock each Day, in Mr. Bourdeaux's Yard, at No, 48, on the Bay.

May 19, 1784.   JOHN MITCHELL.

Thirty Seasoned Negroes

To be Sold for Credit, at Private Sale.

AMONGST which is a Carpenter, none of whom are known to be dishonest.

Also, to be sold for Cash, a regular bred young Negroe Man-Cook, born in this Country, who served several Years under an exceeding good French Cook abroad, and his Wife a middle aged Washer-Woman, (both very honest) and their two Children. Likewise, a young Man a Carpenter.

For Terms apply to the Printer.

Library of Congress/Corbis

An advertisement for a 1784 slave auction.

Hulton-Deutsch Collection/Corbis

THREE AFRICANS ABDUCTED FROM ABYSSINIA (PRESENT-DAY ETHIOPIA),
AWAIT THEIR FATE IN CHAINS.

Corbis-Bettmann

AN AUCTIONEER PREPARES TO SELL A SLAVE TO THE HIGHEST BIDDER. SLAVES WERE OFTEN TAKEN AWAY FROM THEIR FAMILIES AND SOLD AT SUCH AUCTIONS. ARAMINTA'S SISTERS WERE SOLD TO PLANTATION OWNERS WHO TOOK THE GIRLS FAR FROM THEIR FAMILY IN MARYLAND.

Many slave children were taken from their families and sold to people who lived far away. Araminta was one of the fortunate ones who could stay with her parents, but she watched as several of her sisters were dragged away in tears and sold to work in other southern states. She would never see them again.

Edward Brodas had tried to grow tobacco, but his crops did poorly. He made most of his money by renting or selling his slaves. At the age of six, young Araminta was already considered old enough to be "rented out." Slave children were not allowed to go to school because owners worried that educated Blacks might revolt against slavery.

Brodas first rented Araminta to a couple who set her to work as a weaver. They thought she wasn't quick enough, so they gave her the task of wading into a stream to collect muskrats from hunting traps. She caught the measles, and the freezing cold water made her so sick that the couple sent her back to Brodas.

AFRICAN AMERICANS WERE FORCED TO LABOR AT JOBS THAT NO ONE ELSE WANTED TO DO. THESE SLAVES HAD THE DIFFICULT AND BACK-BREAKING JOB OF PICKING COTTON IN THE HOT SOUTHERN CLIMATE.

Corbis-Bettmann

When Araminta recovered, Brodas sent her to another home to do housework and care for a baby. She was whipped for not knowing how to dust furniture or clean floors. She tried to stay up all night to watch the baby, but whenever his crying woke the mother, Araminta was whipped again. The beatings happened so often, Araminta began to prepare for them by finding as many pieces of clothing as she could and wearing them all at once to protect her skin. These brutal beatings still left deep scars on her neck and back. The mother finally sent Araminta back to Brodas when she caught her eating a sugar cube.

Brodas decided Araminta was better suited to outdoor labor. Strong for her size, she could swing an ax well enough to cut wood. At age 11, she began working in the fields with her father, Ben Ross. Ben taught her about the forest. He showed her how to walk without making a sound. He explained which plants could be used for medicine and which ones were good to eat. It seemed as if her father might be teaching Araminta how to survive if she ever ran away.

VIOLENCE WAS A BRUTAL FACT OF LIFE FOR AFRICAN AMERICAN SLAVES, WHO COULD BE PUNISHED SEVERELY WHENEVER AN OWNER WAS DISSATISFIED. FOR THE REST OF HER LIFE, ARAMINTA'S SCARS WERE A TERRIBLE REMINDER OF HER LIFE AS A SLAVE.

Corbis-Bettmann

U.S. Army Military History Institute/Corbis

AFRICAN AMERICAN SLAVES LIVED TOGETHER IN EXTREMELY SMALL QUARTERS, SUCH AS THIS CABIN IN GEORGIA.

U.S. Army Military History Institute/Corbis

TWO RUNAWAY SLAVES POSE FOR A PORTRAIT
IN THE NORTH. SOME AFRICAN AMERICANS
SUCCESSFULLY ESCAPED, BUT THE ROAD TO
FREEDOM WAS A DIFFICULT ONE.

Runaways on the Underground Railroad

One day, when Araminta was a teenager, she saw a slave attempting to run away. His owner chased after him with a whip and finally caught him. Araminta was told to hold the slave while the owner whipped him. She refused and tried to help the slave escape instead.

The furious owner picked up a heavy weight and threw it at the slave. It accidentally hit Araminta on the forehead, crushing her skull. The blow was so severe that she suffered from dizziness and fainting spells for the rest of her life.

The other slaves praised Araminta's courage, and her mother said such a brave young woman should put aside her childhood name. From then on, she became known by her adult name, Harriet.

Usually owners chose whom their slaves would marry. They wanted the slaves to produce strong, healthy children who would be easy to sell at an auction. Edward Brodas believed Harriet's fainting spells would make her a poor mother and did not arrange a marriage for her. So, in 1844, Harriet was able to marry a man she loved, a freed slave named John Tubman.

Harriet worried that she might one day be sold, separating her from John. She asked him to flee north with her so they would both be free, but he refused. He said people in the North captured runaway slaves and shipped them back to the South. He even threatened to tell Edward Brodas if she tried to run away.

Harriet grew ever more afraid of being sold. She was determined to be free, although she knew that most runaways were caught, brutally beaten, and then sold to owners in the deep South — even farther away from freedom. Finally, Harriet convinced three of her brothers to go with her, and they set out for the North. Harriet's brothers were not as brave as she was. Soon after they started out, all four returned to their owner. No one had even noticed they were gone.

Shortly after the attempted escape, Harriet learned that Brodas had in fact sold her to a plantation in the the deep South, where slaves were said to be treated even worse than they were treated in Maryland. She had heard of a woman in town who helped other runaways. Harriet summoned all her courage and went to her.

The woman sent Harriet north to a family who would help her. These people sent her farther north to another family, and they told her of others who could lead her to freedom. Harriet walked through the woods at night between the homes of those who helped her. Other times, she traveled hidden in a small boat or wagon. During the day, her helpers hid her in a barn or cellar.

HENRY "BOX" BROWN RISES OUT OF A SHIPPING CRATE AMID MEN FROM THE UNDERGROUND RAILROAD. BROWN SHIPPED HIMSELF FROM THE SOUTH IN A CRATE TO ESCAPE SLAVERY.

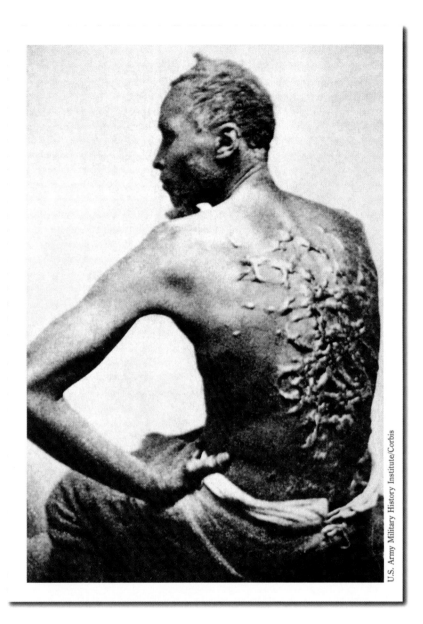

U.S. Army Military History Institute/Corbis

A FORMER SLAVE DISPLAYS TERRIBLE SCARS.
RUNAWAY SLAVES WERE SEVERELY PUNISHED
BY THEIR MASTERS IF THEY WERE CAPTURED.

AMERICANS, BOTH BLACK AND WHITE, ORGANIZED THE UNDERGROUND
RAILROAD TO HELP SLAVES ESCAPE. THIS MAP SHOWS SOME OF THE
ROUTES THAT LED THOUSANDS OF AFRICAN AMERICANS TO FREEDOM.

Harriet and other runaway slaves were said to travel on an imaginary railroad called the *Underground Railroad*. This was a code name for the secret escape route of the slaves. They stopped at "train stations," or the homes of the people who would help them along the way. There were "conductors" on the railroad, the people who carried the slaves in wagons, carts, and boats from one station to another. About 3,000 conductors eventually helped more than 100,000 slaves escape to freedom.

Traveling on the Underground Railroad, Harriet finally crossed into Pennsylvania, where slavery was illegal. It was 1849, and she had spent nearly 30 years as a slave. That was now behind her. Harriet began to make plans to rescue her family. She got a job in a Philadelphia hotel kitchen and saved money to pay for a secret trip to the South.

Harriet attended the meetings of a group that helped runaways through the Underground Railroad and met a man named William Still. He was a free African American who devoted his life to helping slaves escape to freedom. Still learned that Harriet's sister Mary was about to be sold. They formed a plan to get her to Baltimore on the Underground Railroad. Mary, her husband, and their two children sailed north to Baltimore, hidden in a small boat. Harriet sneaked south to meet them. A week later, they were all free.

Schomburg Center for Research in Black Culture

HARRIET'S FRIEND, WILLIAM STILL, WROTE A BOOK CALLED *THE UNDERGROUND RAILROAD.*

Then the Fugitive Slave Act of 1850 was passed, stating that runaways in the North must be arrested and returned to their owners. Anyone who helped the slaves would be fined $1,000 and sent to jail. It was no longer safe to stop in Pennsylvania, so conductors began to take their passengers on to Canada.

After rescuing her sister's family, Harriet successfully transported her brother James and two friends to freedom with the help of Thomas Garrett, the most famous of the Underground Railroad "stationmasters." In 1851, Harriet planned a third trip back to Maryland for her husband John. When she arrived, she found he had married another woman. Harriet was hurt but refused to waste her efforts, so she led more slaves through the Underground Railroad.

Harriet soon became famous. Southern slaves knew about Moses, who in ancient times had freed his people from slavery in Egypt. They sang about him in *spirituals*. People began to call Harriet "Moses" because she also led her people from slavery.

On her fourth trip south, Harriet planned to help only her brother and his wife. Instead, she brought 11 passengers safely to Philadelphia and on to Canada. On her next trip, Harriet led nine more slaves to freedom. One man was so scared, he wanted to turn back. Harriet feared that if he were threatened, he might name those who had helped him. She pulled out a gun, pointed it at his head, and said, "Dead folks tell no tales." He agreed to continue onward.

In June 1857, Harriet made her most daring trip of all to free her parents. She purchased a train ticket and traveled in daylight, even though a reward of $40,000 had been offered for her capture. Her parents were too old to walk all the way to Canada, so Harriet put a board across an old set of wheels to make a wagon. She hitched it to a plow horse and rode them out. The three finally arrived at Thomas Garrett's home. He fed them, praised her parents for raising such a brave daughter, and gave them money to get to Canada.

Corbis-Bettmann

HARRIET TUBMAN (FAR LEFT) POSES WITH A GROUP OF AFRICAN AMERICAN FUGITIVES WHOM SHE HELPED ESCAPE FROM SLAVERY.

Schomburg Center for Research in Black Culture

HARRIET'S AUBURN, NEW YORK, HOME IS NOW AN HISTORICAL LANDMARK. MANY PEOPLE VISIT THE SITE EACH YEAR TO LEARN MORE ABOUT THE UNDERGROUND RAILROAD.

Canada was too cold for Harriet's elderly parents, who were used to the warm climate of the South. The family moved to Auburn, New York, where Harriet bought a home from William Henry Seward. Seward, the former Governor of New York and a member of the U.S. Senate. Seward was one of Harriet's greatest admirers and a life-long friend. He wanted to give her a small home on his land in Auburn, but Harriet refused to accept charity. Instead, he sold her the house, asking only small payments. Harriet would live there for the next 50 years, and the house still stands today.

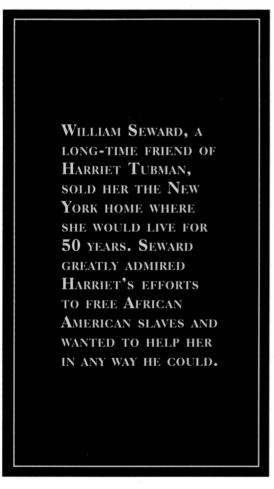

WILLIAM SEWARD, A LONG-TIME FRIEND OF HARRIET TUBMAN, SOLD HER THE NEW YORK HOME WHERE SHE WOULD LIVE FOR 50 YEARS. SEWARD GREATLY ADMIRED HARRIET'S EFFORTS TO FREE AFRICAN AMERICAN SLAVES AND WANTED TO HELP HER IN ANY WAY HE COULD.

Corbis-Bettmann

A Scout and a Heroine

Many Americans believed that slavery was wrong and should not be tolerated. Harriet worked closely with many *abolitionists* who wanted to end slavery. Among them was Frederick Douglass, one of the most influential African Americans of his day. Douglass, too, had been a runaway slave. He was a famous speaker and began a newspaper, *The North Star*, dedicated to the abolitionists' cause.

Then, in 1857, something happened to further separate those who were for slavery and those who were against it.

Dred Scott was a slave, owned by an officer in the United States Army. The army transferred the officer from the slave state of Missouri to the free state of Illinois, and he took Scott with him when he moved. When the army sent the officer back to Missouri, Scott returned there with him.

After his master died, Scott sued the United States government, claiming that he had lived in a free state and was therefore a free man. The case went before the United States Supreme Court. In the Dred Scott decision, the majority of the court (seven out of nine judges) ruled that Scott was still a slave and not a U.S. citizen. Since he was not a citizen, he had no constitutional rights. The decision stated that African Americans, "being of an inferior order," had "no rights which a White man was bound to respect."

This decision angered many Americans. Among them was a young lawyer from Illinois named Abraham Lincoln. He opposed the Dred Scott decision in his campaign speeches for Senator, and then for President. Lincoln argued that if the courts can deny rights to African Americans, they might one day deny them to other groups as well. He reminded voters that the Constitution says "all men are created equal."

William Rubal/AP Wide World Photos

FREDERICK DOUGLASS WAS AN INFLUENTIAL VOICE IN THE FIGHT TO END SLAVERY AND ESTABLISH RIGHTS FOR AFRICAN AMERICANS.

Archive Photos

ABOLITIONIST JOHN BROWN DEDICATED HIS LIFE TO ENDING SLAVERY IN THE UNITED STATES. HE WAS SENTENCED TO DEATH FOR ORGANIZING A RAID TO PROTEST SLAVERY IN 1859.

Other Americans, many of them White, also opposed the decision. Abolitionist John Brown was another of Harriet's friends. In fact, it was he who nicknamed her "General Tubman" because of her bravery in the battle against slavery. Brown realized that peaceful attempts to abolish slavery were not working, so he led a raid on the United States *Arsenal* at Harpers Ferry, in West Virginia. He was later hung for *treason*.

Abraham Lincoln's stand against slavery turned slave owners against him. When he was elected President in 1860, 11 southern states withdrew from the United States to form the *Confederate States of America*.

ABRAHAM LINCOLN OPPOSED THE DRED SCOTT DECISION. IN HIS CAMPAIGN SPEECHES FOR THE PRESIDENCY, HE SAID THE SUPREME COURT SHOULD NOT HAVE DENIED EQUAL RIGHTS TO AFRICAN AMERICANS.

In December of the same year, Harriet made her final trip on the Underground Railroad. "General" Tubman had been fighting her war against slavery in the way she knew best. She had spent 11 years leading slaves to freedom, and her reputation had spread, but now she was needed elsewhere.

Archive Photos

The American Civil War began in April 1861. Harriet spent the next three years working for the *Union Army*. Massachusetts sent her to help the freed slaves. She arranged for the women to support themselves by doing the soldiers' laundry. At the same time, thousands of African American men joined the Union Army. Not all Whites agreed that African Americans should be involved in combat. In fact, the army only paid them half the salary White soldiers were paid.

As the battles continued, more and more men were wounded, so Harriet set up field hospitals. She was tireless in her nursing efforts, helping both White and African American soldiers. When the army needed information, Harriet formed a group of African American *scouts*. Using her skills from the Underground Railroad, she led them through the woods behind enemy lines. They gathered information about enemy positions and recruited slaves who wanted to leave their masters.

Later Harriet helped plan a raid into Confederate territory. A union force of 300 freed slaves began shelling Confederate outposts from three gunboats. When it was over, they had freed 756 more slaves, destroyed millions of dollars worth of Confederate supplies, and walked away without harm.

Corbis-Bettmann

AFRICAN AMERICANS PLAYED AN IMPORTANT ROLE IN THE WAR TO END SLAVERY. THEY MADE UP MORE THAN 10 PERCENT OF THE UNION ARMY TOWARD THE END OF THE WAR.

Corbis-Bettmann

WOUNDED CIVIL WAR SOLDIERS IN VIRGINIA AWAIT HELP. MORE THAN
140,000 MEN WERE KILLED DURING THE FOUR YEARS OF THE AMERICAN
CIVIL WAR, AND ANOTHER 280,000 WERE WOUNDED.

Corbis-Bettmann

HARRIET SPENT THREE YEARS WITH THE
UNION ARMY DURING THE AMERICAN CIVIL
WAR BUT WAS NEVER PAID FOR HER EFFORTS.

Harriet cooked the last meal before battle for Colonel Robert Shaw and the 54th Massachusetts Regiment. In the first major battle using Black troops, they set out to raid Fort Wagner in South Carolina. Shaw led his men to the top of the fort but was shot and killed. His troops kept charging into the enemy fire. Knowing they were doomed, they bravely continued. The battle and their lives were lost, but the regiment had proven its courage.

After three years of war, Harriet was tired and penniless. She had been sent into the thick of combat for three years, but the army never paid her. After the war was over, despite the pleas of army leaders, the government refused to offer her the pension given to others who had served their country. In 1864, she went back to Auburn, haunted by what she had seen during the war. She knew her parents needed her.

THE 54TH MASSACHUSETTS REGIMENT, CONSISTING ONLY OF BLACK TROOPS, ATTACKS FORT WAGNER IN CHARLESTON, SOUTH CAROLINA.

Corbis-Bettmann

Mrs. Harriet Davis, Leader of Her People

The Confederate Army surrendered on April 9, 1865. The war to end slavery was over, and the Union had won. Only five days later, the man who led that fight, President Abraham Lincoln, was shot. He died the next morning. Harriet knew there was much more he could have done to help her people. After his *assassination*, she became even more determined to do whatever she could for African Americans.

While nursing the wounded during the war, Harriet had cared for a young patient named Nelson Davis. Six years later, he visited her in Auburn, and soon he asked her to marry him. In 1869, she became Mrs. Harriet Davis. Nelson looked strong and healthy, but he was never completely well after the war. Nonetheless, they had a happy, peaceful marriage for the next 19 years until Nelson died in 1888.

In the years that followed the Civil War, Harriet, with the help of her neighbors in Auburn, began a program to assist African Americans in need. Most of her money came from raising vegetables and selling them door to door. Everyone knew and respected her. The people of Auburn often welcomed her into their homes to tell the stories of her adventures.

Corbis-Bettmann

African Americans were free after the Civil War, but they still faced many challenges. It was difficult to earn a living and to feed and shelter their families. Harriet continued to do what she could to help her people live better lives long after slavery was abolished.

Archive Photos

HARRIET TUBMAN RESPECTED THE WORK OF
SUFFRAGIST SUSAN B. ANTHONY, ANOTHER
WOMAN WHO BELIEVED IN EQUAL RIGHTS FOR
ALL AMERICANS — BLACK OR WHITE, MALE
OR FEMALE.

Harriet also began a fund-raising campaign to start schools for the freed slaves. A close friend, Sarah Hopkins Bradford, wrote Harriet's biography. The book, *Harriet Tubman: Leader of Her People,* earned $1,200 when it was published. The money was used to support Harriet's parents, to assist the sick and hungry who came to her, and to help set up schools for freed African Americans in the South.

Harriet also wanted to open a home for elderly African Americans. She had no money, but that had never stopped her. At an auction to sell 25 acres near her house, she bid $1,450 and won. Then she convinced the bank to loan her the money to pay for it. Later Harriet gave the land to an African American church to build a nursing home, which opened in 1908. The nursing home, called the Harriet Tubman Home for the Aged, is still in existence today.

Harriet also found a new cause to support. She strongly believed all people should be treated equally, regardless of gender or race. Harriet realized that women, like African Americans, did not have the same rights as White men. After all, the government refused to recognize her Civil War efforts because she was a Black woman.

The 15th Amendment had granted Black men the right to vote in 1870, but women of all races were still denied this privilege. Susan B. Anthony, a leader of the *suffrage movement,* believed the rights guaranteed to American citizens should be the same for everyone. Harriet joined the suffragists and became friends with Susan. Each respected the other's achievements and dedication to equal rights for all Americans. The suffrage Amendment to the Constitution was not ratified until 1920, and neither Harriet nor Susan lived to see women achieve the right to vote.

In 1911, Harriet moved into the nursing home she had helped open three years earlier. She died there on March 10, 1913, at the age of 93.

A tremendous crowd of friends and admirers came to Harriet's funeral. A bugler played *taps* as all the local war veterans stood at attention to honor the courageous heroine. Harriet's friend Frederick Douglass had died 18 years earlier. A man named Booker T. Washington had taken over his role as spokesman for African Americans. Booker came to New York from Alabama to speak at Harriet's funeral. He also dedicated a memorial in her honor.

Harriet Tubman was known by many names during her lifetime. Little Araminta Ross had been badly beaten as a slave child and vowed to do everything she could in the future to end the injustice of slavery. As she grew older, she was given the adult name of Harriet. Her people called her Moses because she freed slaves as the biblical hero had. Others called her General, both for her bravery on the Underground Railroad and her contributions during the American Civil War.

Harriet Ross Tubman spent a lifetime caring for others and working for the freedom of her people, yet she died without great fame, honor, or reward. Today she is remembered, by her people and by her nation, as an African American woman who led the fight for freedom.

Schomburg Center for Research in Black Culture

HARRIET REACHED THE AGE OF 93. HER LONG LIFE WAS DEDICATED TO THE WELFARE OF HER PEOPLE.

Timeline

1820 or 1821	Harriet Tubman, then named Araminta Ross, is born.
1826	Edward Brodas sends six-year-old Araminta to work as a weaver.
1831	Araminta works with her father, Ben Ross, in the woods.
1833	Araminta is permanently injured when a weight thrown at another slave accidentally strikes her on the forehead.
1844	Araminta, now named Harriet, marries John Tubman.
1849	Harriet successfully escapes to the North via the Underground Railroad.
1850	The Fugitive Slave Act is passed.
1857	The Supreme Court files the Dred Scott decision. Harriet buys a home in Auburn, New York, from William Seward. She will live there for the next 50 years.
1850–1860	Harriet makes 19 trips on the Underground Railroad to help more than 300 slaves to freedom.
1861	The American Civil War begins. Harriet joins the the Union Army.
1864	Harriet returns to Auburn to care for her parents.
1865	The Civil War ends, and slaves are freed. Abraham Lincoln is assassinated.
1869	Harriet marries Nelson Davis.
1888	Nelson Davis dies.
1908	The Harriet Tubman Home for the Aged opens.
1911	Harriet moves into the nursing home.
1913	Harriet Ross Tubman Davis dies at the age of 93.

Glossary

abolitionists
Individuals who worked to abolish, or end, slavery in the United States during the 19th century.

African American
An American whose ancestors came from Africa.

arsenal
A place where weapons are manufactured or stored.

assassination
The sudden murder of an individual, usually a politician or otherwise famous person.

Confederate States of America
The 11 states that withdrew from the United States prior to the beginning of the American Civil War.

scouts
Individuals who explore an area; during war, scouts uncover information about the enemy.

slave
A person who is forced to serve another without pay.

spirituals
Religious songs written by African American slaves in the southern United States.

suffrage movement
Political action and protests undertaken to achieve the right to vote for women.

taps
The military bugle call played at funerals and memorial services to honor the dead.

treason
The act of betraying one's government.

Underground Railroad
The system by which abolitionists helped fugitive slaves reach freedom in the North or Canada.

Union Army
The army of the the United States (the northern states) during the American Civil War.

Index

For Further Information

Books

Bentley, Judith. *Dear Friend: Thomas Garrett and William Still, Collaborators on the Underground Railroad.* New York, NY: Cobblehill Books, 1997.

Bradford, Sarah H. *Harriet Tubman: Moses of Her People.* Bedford, MA: Applewood Books, 1994.

Mosher, Kiki. *Learning about Bravery from the Life of Harriet Tubman.* New York, NY: Powerkids Press, 1997.

Web Sites

http://www.nyhistory.com/harriettubman/website.htm

http://www.undergroundrailroad.com

About the Author

Don Troy was born and raised in Boston, Massachusetts. He received his Ph.D. from Boston University in 1971 and was certified as a Total Family Therapist by Boston Family Institute in 1973.

He taught at Stonehill College in Massachusetts from 1963 to 1973. Moving to California in 1973, he spent four years as the director of a national trade association for marriage and family educators and counsellors.